MY COMMUNION BOOK

A child's guide to Holy Communion
Second edition

Diana Murrie
Illustrations by Craig Cameron

CHURCH HOUSE
PUBLISHING

How to use this book

This book aims to help children engage with the service of Holy Communion, in ways that are appropriate to them.

It is designed to be used alongside whichever version of *Common Worship* your congregation is using. It can be used initially as a sharing book, adult and child reading together, but children may want to use it at times on their own.

Key words and texts are given in full or in part and children should be encouraged to join in with everyone else.

Before the service

Talk to the children about what happens during the service, using this book if possible.

Talk with them about the church building, its features and furnishings and how they will be used. Use the vocabulary of your tradition - cup, plate, chalice, paten ...

Talk about the people who help during the service and what they do - sidesperson, organist or worship leader, vicar ...

Give the children things to look out for and identify - symbols, colours, windows, banners ...

Explain the different postures - praying, standing, sitting, going forward to receive Communion or a blessing.

Tell the children of the need for the quiet moments, when people talk to God in their hearts. And that they will need to speak to you in whispers!

In the service

Sit where the children can see.

During the service, answer any questions briefly, following up with fuller explanations at the end.

Use the pictures and words from the service in this book to give children the opportunity to think and reflect. Some suggestions are included in the text.

Have a supply of drawing and colouring materials, books and similar for the sermon slot, or times when a quiet activity is appropriate. Keep these things in a special 'church' bag, which is kept for church days.

Be realistic and flexible in your expectations of the children's responses.

Enjoy yourselves!

Why do we come together?

We come to celebrate and remember the Big Story.

God created our world and loved it so much that he sent his Son, Jesus, to be born and live like one of us.

He died on the cross for our sins and rose again, so we might be forgiven and have everlasting life.

We also come to celebrate and remember our own stories - your story about you, my story about me, our hopes and fears, our joy and sadness.

We are all special to God, who knows all our stories!

What part of your story is important today?

Jesus invites us through bread and wine to share, remember and celebrate his death, his rising and his coming again.

What other things do we celebrate?

The Gathering

God calls us together

to worship

to sing

to say sorry

to be forgiven

to listen to his word

to pray for others

to break and share bread

to go out to love
and serve him.

We sing loudly.

We listen carefully.

We pray quietly.

The Greeting

We may hear: **The Lord be with you.**

We say:
and also with you.

Prayer of Preparation

Preparation means 'getting ready'. We ask God to help us worship him.

We may say:

Almighty God,
to whom all hearts are open,
all desires known,
and from whom no secrets are hidden:
cleanse the thoughts of our hearts
by the inspiration of your Holy Spirit,
that we may perfectly love you,
and worthily magnify your holy name;
through Christ our Lord.

Amen.

Prayers of Penitence

We say sorry to God for all the wrong things we have done and said.

What do you want to say sorry to God for today?

The Absolution

We are glad that God
promises to forgive us.

We may hear:

Almighty God,
who forgives all who truly repent,
have mercy upon you,
pardon and deliver you from all your sins,
confirm and strengthen you in all goodness
and keep you in life eternal;
through Jesus Christ our Lord.

We say: Amen.

Gloria in Excelsis

This begins with the song
the angels sang at Christmas.

We may say or sing:

Glory to God in the highest,
And peace to his people on earth ...

We praise God
for his glory.

What do you think 'glory' is?

The Collect

The Collect is a special prayer for today.

We listen quietly.

At the end of the prayer we say: **Amen.**

Readings

God speaks to us through the words of the Bible. We listen carefully.

We may hear: **This is the word of the Lord.**

We say:
Thanks be to God.

Gospel Reading

We stand to listen to
a story about Jesus,
or a story Jesus told.

We may hear:
**Hear the Gospel of our
Lord Jesus Christ ...**

We say: **Glory to you, O Lord.**

After the Gospel reading we may hear:
This is the Gospel of the Lord.

We say: **Praise to you, O Christ.**

The Sermon

We listen quietly to the talk.

The Creed

We stand to say the really
important things about what
we believe.

We may say:

We believe in one God,
the Father, the Almighty,
maker of heaven and earth ...

We believe in one Lord,
Jesus Christ,
the only Son of God ...

We believe in the Holy Spirit,
The Lord, the giver of life ...

Amen.

There are several ways
we can say the Creed.

Can you find out about any others?

Prayers of Intercession

This is the time when
we pray for others.

We pray for

- the Church throughout
  the world

- the world in which we live

- the people who live near us

- people who are ill, in pain,
  sad, lonely, or in need

- and we remember people
  who have died.

What can you pray for today?

Who can you pray for today?

We may hear: **Lord in your mercy**
We say: **Hear our prayer.**

We cannot know how our prayers
will be answered, but we know
that every prayer is heard.

We may hear: **Merciful Father,**

We say: **accept these prayers
for the sake of your Son,
our Saviour Jesus Christ.
Amen.**

The Peace

God asks us all to love each other, as he loves us. The Peace helps us to show our love. People may greet one another at this time.

We may hear: **The peace of the Lord be always with you**

We say: **and also with you.**

Preparation of the Table

The collection may be taken at this time.

The Communion table is prepared. Bread and wine are placed on the table. Watch carefully to see what happens.

The Eucharistic Prayer

Jesus shared the Last Supper with his disciples. He gave thanks for bread and wine and shared the meal with them. Jesus told his friends to remember him whenever they shared bread and wine. We are going to do this today.

We may hear: **The Lord be with you**
We say: **and also with you.**
or
We may hear: **The Lord is here.**
We say: **His Spirit is with us.**

We may hear: Lift up your hearts.
We say: We lift them to the Lord.

We may hear: Let us give thanks to the
                    Lord our God.
We say: It is right to give thanks and praise.

Listen for the Sanctus:

We say: Holy, holy, holy Lord,
              God of power and might,
              heaven and earth are
              full of your glory.
              Hosanna in the highest.

The Lord's Prayer

We say together the prayer that Jesus taught us.
It begins **Our Father** ...

There are two ways of saying the prayer.

Our Father in heaven,
hallowed be your name,
your kingdom come,
your will be done,
on earth as in heaven.
Give us today our daily bread.
Forgive us our sins
as we forgive those who sin against us.
Lead us not into temptation
but deliver us from evil.
For the kingdom, the power,
and the glory are yours
now and for ever.
Amen.

How are they different?
How are they the same?

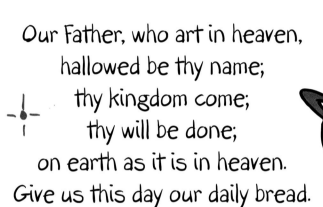

Our Father, who art in heaven,
hallowed be thy name;
thy kingdom come;
thy will be done;
on earth as it is in heaven.
Give us this day our daily bread.
And forgive us our trespasses,
as we forgive those who trespass against us.
And lead us not into temptation;
but deliver us from evil.
For thine is the kingdom,
the power and the glory,
for ever and ever.
Amen.

Breaking of the Bread

We remember Jesus sharing bread with his disciples and we get ready to do the same.

We hear: **We break this bread to share in the body of Christ.**

We say: **Though we are many, we are one body, because we all share in one bread.**

Jesus is sometimes called the Paschal Lamb. Can you find out what paschal means?

John the Baptist called Jesus the Lamb of God.
Can you find this in your Bible?
(John 1.29)

Agnus Dei means Lamb of God.

We may say: **Lamb of God,**
you take away the sin of the world...

or:

Jesus, Lamb of God,
have mercy on us ...

Giving of Communion

We get ready to receive communion or a blessing.

We say: **Amen.**

As you see all the people go forward, remember that they are your brothers and sisters in Christ, the family of God where you live and a part of the worldwide Church.

Sit quietly and think of all that you have said and heard today.

What is really, really important about it?

Look back through this book. Think about what you have found out today. Here are some questions to start you off.

What made you think the most?

What did you like best?

What did you find hard?

What made you glad?

Prayer after Communion

We may say:

Almighty God,
we thank you
for feeding us ...

The Dismissal
means 'sending out'.

We receive a blessing.
We say: **Amen.**

We may hear: **Go in peace to love
and serve the Lord.**

We say: **In the name of Christ. Amen.**

or

We may hear: **Go in the peace of Christ.**

We say: **Thanks be to God.**

We go home, knowing that God is always with us,
wherever we are, whatever we do.

After the service

Answer any questions. Encourage the children to return their books and service sheets, tidy the kneelers and join in any post-worship coffee, orange and biscuits, to meet other members of the church. Now is the time to go and look at the altar or table, chancel and vestry.

Talk about the service. What was enjoyable and memorable? Tell the children what you enjoyed.

During the week

Encourage the development of any debate, reflection or enquiry begun during or after the service. Play church at home. Let the children use a variety of art and craft materials to make things that reflect their ideas, e.g. collage pictures, clay models, word pictures or poems.

Talk positively about worship. Tell the children how much you value worshipping with them. Make going to church a special event.

Try to create an atmosphere where children can share freely their response to worship and to God, whenever it seems appropriate to them.

Encourage children to talk to God.

Tell them you pray for them.

Pray together as a family or a smaller group, whenever it feels comfortable and right. Table grace, birthdays and the beginnings and ends of journeys are all good times. Have a home 'intercessions' book or noticeboard where concerns can be noted. Then pray about them and use them in Sunday church prayers.

Not all children respond to worship and God-talk in the same way. Be sensitive to difference.

Follow-on activities for families and children's groups

Make a scrapbook or collage picture about 'People who go to My Church' - the flower arrangers, musicians, churchwardens. Who are they and what do they do? Arrange for the congregation to see the finished article.

Ask the children what jobs they would like to do at church and find out who could help them do these jobs.

Devise a church trail for families to find out more about the building.

Help the children to write and illustrate 'A Children's Guide to Our Church'.

Church House Publishing
Church House
Great Smith Street
London
SW1P 3AZ

ISBN 978-0-7151-4225-7
Second edition

Eighth impression 2016

Published 2002 by National Society Enterprises Ltd

Designed and typeset by Craig Cameron

Printed by Ashford Colour Press Ltd, Gosport, Hampshire